root theatre e...

Root Theatre and Ros Terry ...

BIRD

by Laura Lomas

Bird was first performed at Derby Theatre Studio on
10 October 2014

BIRD

by Laura Lomas

CAST

LEAH   **Amaka Okafor**

CREATIVE TEAM

Director	**Jane Fallowfield**
Producer	**Ros Terry**
Designer	**Joanna Scotcher**
Lighting Designer	**Prema Mehta**
Sound Designer	**Becky Smith**
Assistant Designer	**Daisy Young**
Production and Technical Stage Manager	**Hannah Blamire**
Press Representative	**Alex Gammie**
Outreach Associate and Assistant Director	**Charley Miles**
Re-Lighter	**Ben Cowens**
Movement Director	**Coral Messam**

BIOGRAPHIES

Ben Cowens (RE-LIGHTER)
Ben Cowens trained at the Academy of Live and Recorded Arts in stage management and technical theatre specialising in lighting design for theatre, events & dance. Since graduating he has designed productions internationally and re-lit productions around the United Kingdom. Lighting design work includes *iCoDaCo* (Aberystwyth Arts Centre/ Cardiff Dance House/Suzanne Dellal Centre); *Showtime* (Bridlington Spa); *The Domino Heart* (Finborough); *We Happy Few* (New Diorama); *Conversations with Dystonia* (The Place); *How to Find Us* (Soho); *The Story Project 5* (Arcola); *Is it Getting Cold in Here?…* (Theatre503). Relight work includes *My People* (tour of Wales); *Speed*, *The Snow Spider* (Tristan Bates); *Snap. Catch. Slam* (Plough Arts Centre). You can find more information and up and coming work at www.bencowens.co.uk

Jane Fallowfield (DIRECTOR)
Jane Fallowfield is Literary Associate at Talawa Theatre Company and Director on Attachment at Clean Break. She has directed *Fingertips* by Suhayla El Bushra (Clean Break); *The Only Way is Chelsea's* by Frazer Flintham (York Theatre Royal/Soho); *Cosmic* by Tom Wells (Hull Truck); *Where's My House?* by Frazer Flintham (New Vic Stoke/Islington Community Theatre) and *Lagan* by Stacey Gregg (Ovalhouse). Assistant directing includes National Theatre, Royal Court, National Theatre and RSC.

Laura Lomas (WRITER)
Laura Lomas is from Derby. In 2009 she was a member of Paines Plough/Channel 4's Future Perfect Scheme and in 2011 she completed an attachment at the National Theatre Studio. Plays include *Blister* (Paines Pough/Royal Welsh College of Music and Drama); *Open Heart Surgery* (Theatre Uncut); *Come to Where I'm From* (Paines Plough); *Some Machine* (Paines Plough/Rose Bruford); *The Island* (Nottingham Playhouse/Det Norske Oslo); *Us Like Gods* (Hampstead, Heat and Light); *Gypsy Girl* (Paines Plough Later at Soho) and *Wasteland* (New Perspectives/Derby Theatre; shortlisted for the Brian Way Award). Radio plays include *My Boy* (BBC Radio 4 Afternoon Play; Bronze SONY Award for best radio drama) and *Lucy Island* (BBC Radio 3). Laura's screen work includes *Rough Skin* (Touchpaper/Channel 4; shortlisted for Best British Short at British Independent Film Awards and Raindance Film Festival). She has also written two episodes of *Glue* (E4/Eleven Films), and is developing a feature film with Element Pictures. Laura is currently under commission to BBC Radio 4, Manchester Royal Exchange, and joint commission to Clean Break and Birmingham Rep. She was a MacDowell Colony Fellow 2013, and a Yaddo Fellow 2014.

Prema Mehta (LIGHTING DESIGNER)
Prema Mehta trained at the Guildhall School of Music and Drama, and
has since designed the lighting for over one hundred drama and dance
productions. Designs for drama productions include *The Great
Extension* (Theatre Royal Stratford East); *Snow Queen* (Derby Theatre);
The Husbands (UK tour); *Calcutta Kosher* (Arcola); *Fourteen* (Watford
Palace Theatre); *The Royal Duchess* (The Broadway); *The Electric Hills*
(Liverpool Everyman). Designs for dance productions include *Hercules*
(New Art Club at Nottingham Playhouse/UK tour); *Penguin Café* in
collaboration with The London College of Fashion (Cochrane); *Jugni*
(UK tour); *Bells* (Mayor of London's Showtime event); *Sufi Zen* (Royal
Festival Hall); *Dhamaka* (O2 Arena) and *Maaya* (Westminster Hall). She
also collaborated with an artist to create a glass, mirror and light
installation for a project called *Shared Memories* (Arcola). Further
details are available at www.premamehta.com

Charley Miles (ASSISTANT DIRECTOR)
Charley Miles is a writer and director from North Yorkshire. She
graduated from Warwick University in 2012. Assistant directing includes
A Midsummer Night's Dream for Sprite Productions and *The Only Way is
Chelsea's* for Root Theatre. Writing includes *Take the Wind* (radio) for
Heads Together Productions. She was recently on attachment to the
North Wall Arts Centre, where she developed *fallow field*.

Amaka Okafor (LEAH)
Amaka Okaafor has been seen in *Glasgow Girls* (National Theatre of
Scotland/Stratford East); *The Snow Queen* (Unicorn/Indian tour/Trestle);
Flathampton (Northampton Royal & Derngate); *Branded*, *24 Hour Plays*
(Old Vic); six productions at the Unicorn as part of their ensemble
company; *Dr Korczak's Example* (Manchester Royal Exchange/Arcola);
Sabbat (The Dukes, Lancaster); *The Bacchae* (National Theatre of
Scotland); *Tracy Beaker Gets Real* (Nottingham Playhouse/national tour);
Stamping Shouting and Singing Home (Polka); *Robin Hood & The Babes in
the Wood*, *When Brecht Met Stanislavsky* (Salisbury Playhouse). Television
includes: *Grandpa in my Pocket* (CBBC), *Doctors* and *The Bill*.

Joanna Scotcher (DESIGNER)
Joanna Scotcher received the Whatsonstage 'Best Set Designer' Award
for her site-specific design of *The Railway Children*, which went on to
win the Olivier award for Best Entertainment in 2011. Joanna was
trained at the Royal Shakespeare Company. From this classical initiation
in stage design, her design projects have taken her from performances
on lakes, through journeys under forgotten London, to games in Royal
Palaces. As well as her theatrical stage design, her work specialises in
the world of immersive performance and site-responsive design,
inhabiting spaces from the epic to the intimate. Her design work has

been exhibited at the V&A Museum's From *Gaga to Gormley* exhibition. Recent work includes *Hopelessly Devoted* by Kate Tempest (Paines Plough); *Pests* by Vivienne Franzmann (Clean Break/Royal Court); *Antigone* by Roy Williams (Pilot Theatre) and *A Harlem Dream* (Young Vic/Dance Umbrella). Joanna forms part of the multi-award-winning theatre company LookLeftLookRight as associate designer. For full credits and to view her portfolio please visit: www.joannascotcher.com, Twitter @JoannaScotcher

Becky Smith (SOUND DESIGNER)
Becky Smith studied drama at Exeter University. Sound designs include *Circles* (Birmingham Rep); *Frozen* (Fingersmiths/Birmingham Rep); *Little on the Inside, Billy the Girl, it felt empty when the heart went at first but it's alright now, A Just Act, This Wide Night, Missing Out* (Clean Break); *The Only Way is Chelsea's, Lagan* (Root Theatre); *The Kitchen Sink* (Hull Truck); *The Well and the Badly Loved* (Risking Enchantment); *Cardboard Dad* (Sherman, Cardiff); *Brood* (Stratford East); *Frozen* (Fresh Glory); *The Juniper Tree, Reverence, The Ghost Sonata* (Goat and Monkey). Becky has also worked as a stage manager for companies including ATC, Paines Plough, The Gate, Polka Theatre and Oily Cart.

Ros Terry (PRODUCER)
Ros Terry is the Producer for Clean Break Theatre Company. Ros's independent producing includes the upcoming JMK Award-winning *Far Away* playing at the Young Vic Theatre this November; *Disco Pigs* (Young Vic Theatre) and *Faith, Hope and Charity* (Southwark Playhouse). She is Co-Director of Echo Presents, a producing company she runs with Gabby Vautier, their aim is to develop the audiences of the future, ensuring their work remains challenging and risk-taking as well as accessible and relevant. She also works as a freelance producer with companies including Birdsnest Theatre, Peut-etre Theatre Company and Music for Youth.

Daisy Young (ASSISTANT DESIGNER)
Daisy Young recently graduated from Nottingham Trent University with a degree in Theatre Design and is enjoying the start of her career in theatre. Regularly assisting Jo Scotcher, she continues to learn and hone her skills, accompanying her own freelance design work. February 2014 brought her first realised design project with Carmarthen Youth Opera's performance of *Evita* and since then she has worked with the Welsh Millenium Centre on a new musical for children. She has really enjoyed working on *Bird* with such a great team of inspiring ladies, developing a keen interest in new writing which she hopes to develop further throughout her career.

root theatre

ROOT THEATRE

Root Theatre develops writers, puts on plays and runs outreach workshops.

We work with writers who: have something to say, put their heart on the line to say it, and say it in a distinctive voice.

We want to make work that is political in its subject matter and execution. Work that is provocative and responds to the world around us, and gets more people involved in theatre.

Our track record of discovering new writers and running innovative community projects includes:

The Only Way is Chelsea's by Frazer Flintham (York Theatre Royal/Live Theatre Newcastle/Soho, London) – winner of York Theatre Royal's Takeover commission; *Cosmic* by Tom Wells (Hull Truck/community centres in inner-city Hull and rural East Riding); *Where's My House?* by Frazer Flintham (New Vic Stoke/Islington Community Theatre); *Lagan* by Stacey Gregg (Ovalhouse).

ECHO PRESENTS

Echo Make Things Happen. We work with people, companies and ideas we love. We produce theatre and events that genuinely engage with new and existing audiences with stories that have a relevance to the world we live in.

We believe that theatre should inform and reflect real lives and that it should be accessible to a diverse audience.

Echo's vision is to develop the audiences of the future, ensuring their work remains challenging and risk-taking as well as accessible and relevant to people who are often under-represented in the demographic of theatre-goers.

Projects include: *American Justice* by Richard Vergette at the Arts Theatre West End and the accompanying young people's response project *Finding Playing Space* funded by Awards for All. Echo are currently developing *The Quiet House* by Gareth Farr, working towards a full production in 2015.

For more information go to www.echopresents.com or follow Echo on Twitter @echopresents

THANKS

Laura Lomas would like to thank the following for their support in the research and development of this play:

Shelia Taylor at NWG; Nick McPartlan at Engage; CROP Leeds; Ella Cockbain and Helen Brayley at UCL; Safe and Sound Derby; Lynn Hannah; Anja Nyberg; Laura Butterworth; The National Theatre Studio; Tom Wells; Ros Terry; Amaka Okafor; Rachel Taylor and Jane Fallowfield – for being such an inspiring collaborator, and friend.

BIRD

for my mum, with love

This text went to press before the end of rehearsals and so may differ slightly from the play as performed.

LEAH, *fourteen*

A dilapidated flat in Hartington Street, Derby.

Darkness, then…

Music plays – 'We Found Love' by Rihanna featuring Calvin Harris, it is loud and energised, completely consuming, but it's dissonant, distorted. Beneath it the sound of a heart beating can be heard at irregular off-beats.

On the walls around the flat, shadows of birds are stretched out – moving, struggling or in flight.

Amid the shadows we can make out the figure of LEAH, *she wears a short, tight, sparkly dress beneath a man's oversized jumper. She is sitting on a mattress listening to the music on earphones – it's in her head.*

Suddenly, the heartbeat gets louder, it collides with the music and rises to a crescendo until…

Lights snap up. LEAH *sees us for the first time. She pulls out her earphones and the music cuts. A pause, she looks at us breathless, suddenly exposed.*

Beat.

I know what you're thinking.

Pause.

Don't look at me like that, course I know. I always know, I ain't stupid.

Beat.

You don't think I know? You don't think I see it? Way you give me them eyes…

Thinking 'why don't she just leave? Door's over there'.

Thinking 'look at her, all dressed up, waiting for her boyfriend to come, as if he's gonna come, four in the morning as if he's even coming for her now', thinking I'm stupid, thinking I'm kiddin' myself, thinking I got nothing but air in my head, is that it? Is that what you're thinking?

Beat. LEAH *looks a little bruised.*

Yeah, well… you people don't know shit.

She walks over to her phone and picks it up.

Sammy ain't text me yet.

Beat.

It's okay, I ain't bothered. I only been here like one hour, it ain't a big deal.

She looks at her phone again. Looks back at us.

I was just walking round town for a bit…

And right… I ain't gonna lie, at first… at first I was upset… okay, at first I was thinking bad thoughts, an', an', an' –

At first I was thinking maybe I done something wrong, cus I couldn't remember. I couldn't remember, everything was so… in my head was so…

Her whole body tenses. Beat.

That's why I called him. To talk to him, hear his voice. Calm me… an' at first when he don't pick up, I was thinking shit – what if something happen to him and the idea of it make me panic so bad I could feel my heart beating right in my throat.

That's why I come here. To get my head straight. Sort my thoughts out, stop 'em banging round my head like a fuckin' machine gun going off.

She looks around the room, looks back at us.

I sat on the bed and tried him again, and this time… The phone just go dead.

I know what you're thinking, that he switch it off on me? An' I was thinking it too, cus all of a sudden I start panicking and I'm sat there with my head in my hands, breathing, trying to keep calm, counting to like thirty.

That's when I remember.

'Bout his situation. How he's always like 'Leah, don't be callin' me late.'

Sammy live with his dad in one of them new houses down Sinfin. He don't like it, he wants to get away, he says he's tired of looking after him, he want his own life too, don't he?

Sammy say his dad is weird, say he don't like the phone, don't like people callin' him. Tell me once when him and his dad was in Asda Sammy's phone kept goin' an' his dad start stressin' so bad, he thought he was gonna have a heart attack, right there in the bread aisle, near the baguettes, he swear down.

Beat. She looks down at her phone.

I text him,

Said 'Hey Babe, I don't mean to keep calling you, but just to let you know… I'm here. I'm at the flat.
I'm waiting for you,
I hope you come get me soon.'

She pauses, summing up whether to tell us.

Then I put

'I'm sorry.'

'I love you'

and a kiss.

Beat. She shifts.

He ain't replied to me yet but it's only cus he's busy.

She starts to tidy the flat.

That's the thing with Sammy, he just gotta find the moment, I know what he's like, he's proper, you know… *discreet* can't have no one seeing, can't have no one finding out 'bout this, tonight. Us two. Where we're going.

Cus after tonight, everything be changed. Nothing be the same no more. That's the truth.

Beat. She looks at us.

You don't believe me?

Beat.

Is it? Really? You don't believe me? You think I'm lying to you? You think I'm lying? You want me to prove it?

Beat.

Fine. I'll prove it.

She gets out her phone and starts flicking through it, angrily. She finds a picture and holds it up to us.

See this? This is our flat. Well, not ours exactly, we don't own it, it's Sammy's cousin's, but he say we can stay there, says it ain't a big deal.

It's in London.

An' I know what you're thinking… Like, why you just gonna go somewhere you don't know no one. How d'you know it won't just be shit, but I already said this to Sammy an' he tell me about the area – this place *Wood Green*. It's amazing. I mean properly. I looked it up on the internet and I swear it's got *everything* fucking… Primark, Miss Selfridge… Nando's!

She looks at the picture.

And alright, I ain't stupid, I know it don't look that good *now*. But you lot don't know Sammy, don't know what he's like, how he look after me. He say it's all gonna be fixed up by the time we get there, say I don't have to worry 'bout nothing. He's gonna take care of everything. He say he want me to meet all his friends, say we can start a new life there and I can just leave everything else behind, all the bad stuff that fuck with my head… just
let it
go.

Beat.

Except for Charlie.

Beat.

I ain't forgotten 'bout Charlie.

Beat.

And you lot don't need to look at me like that, as if I forget her, as if I could even for a minute forget her. As if I could do that.

Beat.

We're gonna go get her.

That's what Sammy say. He say we just gotta get there, get settled, sort stuff out, then first minute we can, said we can go back and get her.

Say she can have her own room, say we can make it all nice for her. Say he's even been looking into schools, cus he want it to be proper for her.

See that's how I know. How much he love me, how much he want to be with me, take care of us. How far he go. Even to look after Charlie, cus he know how much she mean. Say we can be a family, together. The three of us.

And you know, sometimes when I think about it. The thought. the
feeling…

is like I can

Hardly
Even
Breathe.

Beat. She looks at us.

That's why I ain't going nowhere till he get here.

Beat. She looks around the room.

Shit. Look at the state of this place. Man, I need to clean it up before he get here.

She picks up a takeaway bag and begins to clean up the old cans and wrappers that litter the flat.

You see this flat. It's where we always come. I know what you're thinking… that it a bit scabby, right? I ain't gonna pretend it ain't, you lot got eyes int you?

It ain't just us that come here. It's others too. Sometimes you turn up and the place is just waste man. Sammy don't like it, it make him angry, he reckons 'some people are born backwards – they ain't got no respect'.

I remember, first time he brought me here, you shoulda seen his face, the look on it.

Cus it was, you know – kinda nasty, like condoms on the floor, and the bedsheets all messed up. It reek up something proper. You walk in the door and this wave come over you, you know, like hot,
in your face.

Sammy look like someone put a needle in his heart, but I just started laughing and he look at me, like I'm off my head but I can't stop, and he goes 'why you laughing for', and his face is kinda angry, but I can't stop, and he's like 'I said why you laughin', Leah' and I'm just 'I can't help it, the room, it reek of farts'.

He stop frownin' then. And for a minute, his eyes go dark, and I think I say something really bad, cus he look kinda angry…

But then he smile.

This big cheesey smile, full of teeth, how he do.

He just go 'Leah you are a funny little Bird'.

And then he take my face, stroke it
gentle
with his

fingers.

An' all the hairs on my body stand on end…

She gets carried away with the feeling. Then…

LEAH's *phone beeps. Beat. She stares at it on the floor a moment. Suddenly anxious. She waits a beat then walks quickly over and picks it up. She looks at it. Breathes.*

Carla.

She chucks it on the floor again.

I don't know why she's texting me for.

To the phone, as if it were Carla.

I ain't got nothing to say to you.

She looks at us again.

I meet her today. She's the *only* one I wanna see. An' I shoulda known what she'd be like, cus she can be harsh, but she does, you know? She got a good heart.

She's my best friend.

Beat, she looks wounded.

Least I thought she was.

Beat. She composes herself.

We're sat on the bench near Sev's park overlooking the pond.

It's where we always go when we don't wanna go school.

Honest, the amount of hours I spent on that bench, should have my arse-shape moulded into it. Big round circles, and a sign sayin' 'Leah's arse was 'ere'.

Carla's stood up, trying to prove to me how she's learned to levitate.

She's just standing on the bench, but she's adamant that she's floating.

The thing about Carla is she talks shit. She can't help it. It's just what she's like. I used to try and say somethin' but I don't bother no more, I just 'llow it.

Beat.

Carla's stood there telling me about this time when she was
four, that she *actually* died

and

alright,
alright,
I ain't gonna lie to you, we've taken a couple, but only a couple.

Carla's mum has these pills, apparently they're 'to help with her
back pain' but Carla reckons she only takes them cus her dad's a
bastard and she can't afford to leave him.

These pills, they've gone to my head, cus I can feel myself
getting lighter, in my fingers and my chest, and I think about
Sammy, about seeing him tonight,
about his hands on my body and my face,
and the way he kiss me and I look at Carla and she's on the
bench dancing round, the world is just spinning, she's still
talking, I'm watching her lips going, and her eyes are massive
and in that moment, I think she is so
Beautiful.

I have this feeling this, overwhelming feeling of
Pure Love.

Like family, like blood, and the sky is massive, and the air is so
fresh, that when I breathe I think my heart is actually stretching,
put my hand on it and it's like I can feel it,
and I want to tell her, I want to tell her everything

about tonight. About me and Sammy, and the flat in Wood
Green. About that I'm scared, about that I'm excited, about
what is happening, inside me, how I'm so full up of this feeling,
this feeling is like, this feeling is…

And then I am,
I am

I'm just talking and it's *pouring* out of me, it's like a river, and
I'm telling her, about Sammy, about how we're going away
together, about Charlie, how we're gonna come get her when
we're sorted. About how we're gonna be a family. Just the three

of us. About how everything is gonna be different, and better and fucking beautiful, for ever and

I see her.

Her face.

She's stopped dancing, climbs down, she's quiet, and her eyes are still massive, but they've switched, they're locked on mine, Two dark stones.

'You got a picture?'

'What?'

she say it again.

'Show me a picture Leah. I wanna know what he looks like.'

I put my hand in my pocket, pull out my phone, flick through my pictures, and hold it up so she can see.

She shifts, as if trying to shake off the memory of something painful.

I ain't gonna tell you what she said to me.

I ain't, you know why I ain't? Cus I don't want you thinking bad of her.

No, no I don't, I ain't like that, I ain't nasty like that. But I swear and I'll say this to you once, and I say it cus I mean it, full-hearted, that if it was the other way round, and if it was her that was me, and me that was her, I would just be fucking happy
for her, you know?

She looks to the window, the sun is getting a bit higher.

Getting lighter. He'll be here soon.

She puts her hands on her upper arms. Squeezes them, as she cradles herself it hurts a bit but she shakes it off. A sudden shudder goes through her whole body.

Man, I gotta get myself ready.

She runs over to her bag, suddenly wired. She starts to turf stuff out of it, with speed and recklessness. She pulls out a toothbrush – still in its packet, shampoo, lip gloss, mascara, some wipes, a packet of sweets. She pays no notice to anything as she empties it over the floor, she's looking for something – finally she pulls out some red nail varnish.

Knew it.

She holds it up to us triumphantly.

She sits down and begins to paint her nails with care. She talks to us as she paints.

Kevin don't let me wear nail varnish, he reckons it 'ain't appropriate for my age'.

I'm like 'yeah, well your face ain't appropriate for my eyes.'

Beat.

I don't say it. Just think it.

Sammy tells me not to listen to him anyway. He say it don't matter what Kevin think, but I can't help it, he stress me out so much… Sammy just look at me all soft and go

'Babe, you don't need to worry. You don't need to do nothing but be beautiful.'

She looks at us.

And then he smile at me.

Sort of cheeky, cus I know, and I know he knows, I know, what he's doing. Trying to wind me up, trying to send me *crazy*.

But in a good way.

And he means it. When he says stuff like that, I know he means it, you know, cus I feel it. Like a tingle right through me, right down.

A pause, she looks at us, summing up whether to tell us or not.

It's like when I first meet him.

She puts her nail varnish down, suddenly energised.

I'm sat on my own outside Nicky's. Me and Carla always go there, Carla knows the guy who works there. Dave or sumin, I don't know, he's like forty. Reckons he gives her free chips cus he bare fancies her. I have to wait outside cus he don't give it her if I'm there.

We're sat on the wall and Carla's trying to eat her chips all sexy like, smiling at him through the window. She get ketchup on her face but I don't tell her. She'd make out like it's my fault, and I can't be arsed with it. I just 'llow it.

Carla's chatting shit, going on 'bout her new hair
saying
'yeah man, since I got a weave everybody fancy me'
she's like,
'The other day some boy stopped me in Westfield and told me I look just like Beyoncé, you know

but white.'

Swear she's been chattin' 'bout it non stop for twenty minutes cus when she say she's thirsty I'm thinking so am I, and I ain't even talking.

She go to the shop to teef a Coke.

That's when it happen.

Music starts to play – very very low 'You Don't Love Me (No, No, No)' by Dawn Penn.

I'm just locked in my own head, I don't even notice at first, at first I'm just eyes in the sky, dreaming of nothin'.

But then I hear the music.

Music plays a bit louder, beneath it the sound of a heartbeat, and birds' wings from before.

It's that song, I recognise it, you know it, cus Mum she always used to sing it in the kitchen, when she was cleaning.

And I'm bopping, I'm winding where I'm sitting, cus I love this song, I love it, I don't even hear the car rolling up behind me till it's there, and there's a voice

It's sort of low, smooth,
gentle

says 'hey'.

The sound of the wings gets louder.

And for some reason, all the skin on my neck go cold.

I turn round.

Wings and heartbeat, louder.

Right round to face it.

Wings and heartbeat.

And that's when I see him, the first time, see

his green eyes, white teeth

Wings and heartbeat.

I feel my heart beating like birds' wings flapping and then

he's asking 'What's your name?'

And he look at me, right *into* me, and so I tell him.

'My name's Leah

Leah Bird.'

Wings, heartbeat.

'*Bird*' he say.

'Bird' I say.

And he smile at me.

He smiles at me.

He smile
At me.

The music stops. LEAH *is a bit overcome.*

Man I swear that smile is etched to the back of my eyelids cus when I close them. That's all I see.

She smiles.

We started seeing each other from then. I tell Carla 'bout him, but she make out like it no big deal. She tell me ninety-three per cent of relationships are most likely to fail in the first six weeks, so I'm best off not getting my hopes up too much.

But inside, you know, inside me it's like hurricanes.

Beat.

He started texting. Nice stuff at first, calling me his baby, and his girl.

She pauses, not sure of whether to tell us.

Then it get ruder.

She is suddenly shy.

Man, I don't know if I should be telling you this…

Beat.

He say stuff. 'Bout *sex*.

And the stuff he say, at first it was like 'No man! That's disgusting!' But I tell Carla and she says it's normal

She knows loads about sex, she's always saying things, like how it's bullshit that you're only supposed to do it with someone you love, and she don't know why people say that, cus the truth is, if you don't do it enough.
You get depressed.

Carla has done it three times.

And when I show her the texts from Sammy, she's just like, 'raa man, you just gotta go with it, I don't even know why you're stressin', it ain't even a big deal.'

But the thought, make me feel weird, like kinda nervous, like my face go tingly and I feel all hot, and dizzy, and I say this to Sammy, and he is so sweet, he says he's sorry, cus he didn't mean to upset me, it's just when he looks at me, all he sees is this

Woman.

Beautiful.

He get carried away. He's sorry, he can't help it, and he won't go chattin' stuff like that again.

But then I think,
Yeah.

After some time I think, yeah.
Look at myself, and I know what he means, cus I am. Fourteen now, I am. Fully grown.

Woman.

Beat.

An' Carla's right, you know, cus I shouldn't have been stressin'. Cus now we do it all the time, and it ain't even a big deal and I love it. Sammy like it all sort of ways on top, from behind –

Beat, she stops abruptly, as if hearing herself.

He take me to parties and show me off as his girlfriend. He buy me fags, booze, *weed*, anything I want.

Beat. She stops again, looks at us. Another beat.

Can I tell you something?

Beat. She hesitates.

I don't always like the parties. I mean, I do, but, just – sometimes.

They can be a bit weird, like some of the girls there, they can be a bit… a bit, sort of…

She can't finish the sentence.

It's like on Friday. Gone midnight.

Me and Sammy, we're stood on the pavement in Cav looking up at this tiny flat. It's dark so you can't see nothing but I swear it reek of ganja, you could smell it from the street.

We go up, second floor. It's busy – I mean really, there must be least forty people all crammed into this tiny room. The music is pure bass, I can feel it all through my body pumpin' in my heart and in my throat.

We're sitting on the sofa. Sammy's got his hand on my leg, being all protective, kissing me and I look up and see this girl, she's staring at me.

I think she fancy Sammy or something cus she just looking at us both, her lips is curling up, she's not dancing she just standing, like she's wasted or on something, and I don't notice at first, cus of the smoke, but then the lights flash up and I see her, her face. Her lipstick's all smudged and smeared across her mouth, and there's these scratches,
huge,
like nails down her cheeks.

Beat.

I never know no one at the parties, but Sammy look after me.

And we dance, at the parties we always dance.

Music starts low – 'We Found Love' by Rihanna featuring Calvin Harris.

He put his hands on me, on my body.

She indicates her hips.

And he pull me close to him, right up next to him, like this.

She shows us.

And we just move, the two of us, like we's the only ones in the room.

Music blasts. Lights change. We are in the middle of a party, shapes of birds chasing round the walls once more. LEAH dances, she lets herself go. There is an energy to her movement, but something's not right.

We watch her for some time, slowly the music begins to distort, and slow. The sound of birds' wings and a heart beating returns, as in the beginning. LEAH starts to cough, quietly at first, and then more violently. The music cuts out, she continues to cough, struggling for breath, it looks like she might be sick. But finally she gets her breath back. She has her hand on the necklace round her throat, she looks at it.

Sammy buys me presents. All sorts, jewellery, earrings, everything, like you wouldn't even believe.

He buy me this necklace.

She holds up her necklace, it has a heart on it.

We only been seeing each other like two weeks when he give it to me, he look at me, touch my face, and he tell me he love me.

That moment, I can tell you, that feeling, all through my body was like sunshine.

Was like the best feeling, was like, was like… When Charlie was first born, and we was scared, cus she come too quickly, and there was only me there in the kitchen with Mum, and we was so worried, cus she was too quiet, and her skin was blue, so I had to hold her to keep her warm and I rubbed her head, softly, and then she was crying, then I was crying, and Mum, we was all just sat there in the kitchen with all the blood there but crying, cus we was so happy.

Was like that moment, was like that all again.

Pause. Then quietly.

I show the necklace to Carla and she laugh at it. She say 'who even is this guy' and she wanna see a picture but I won't show her. She say the necklace is from Poundland or some shit, like she'd even know.

I don't say nothin'.
but I ain't gonna lie, my heart…
it hurt a bit when she say that.

Suddenly, the sound of a car. A blue and red light from the window washes over her. She looks to the window, anxiously. She waits till it's passed. She looks back at us.

Man, I need to eat something before Sammy get here.

She goes over to her bag and starts to rifle through it. She finds out a tin of macaroni cheese. She holds it up.

See this is the shit we keep in our cupboards. Kevin need to go shopping, man. Me and Charlie, we shouldn't be eatin' stuff like this. If Mum was still here, she'd go mental.

She pulls the ring and opens the can, she picks a fork off the floor, goes to eat some, but as she brings it to her mouth, her hand begins to shake violently. A panic spreads across her face, she chucks the fork and the can on the floor.

I ain't hungry.

Beat.

I only picked it up for Sammy. I don't know why. Maybe cus I was rushin' so much.

She looks at it on the floor. She composes herself.

He wouldn't eat it anyways. He's always picky about food. He never eat nothing but take-out.

Beat.

Once we're at his mate's house.

I'm sitting in the middle of this big ugly room.

This is house something out the seventies I swear.
Nasty brown wallpaper.
Mad carpets that make your eyes go like spirals when you look at them.

'Five minutes' that's what Sammy tells me, 'five minutes'.

He's just gotta pick something up for his cousin 'it'd be rude if we didn't say hello.'

Two hours later and we're still sat there. Look around the room and count the men –

one, two, three, four, five

Swear these men are waste, cus it's like two on a Tuesday and they're all just sat around with the curtains closed, getting lean.

Sammy's smoking up.

Look at him, and my belly turn.

He offer me some but I don't smoke it. He knows I'm pissed off cus I keep giving him evil eyes, like –

She shows us.

He's pretending not to notice, thinking I'll just stop if he don't make eye contact.

This old guy sitting next to me, keeps putting his hand on my leg. Swear, he must be stupid, cus I'm thinking, 'Man that's my boyfriend over there. Can you see him or has your eyesight gone with your looks?'

She kisses her teeth.

Sammy don't say nothing, so I let it go. Must be cus he's old.

'Nother hour goes past, and I'm 'bout ready to walk myself home, when Sammy starts chipping in about me going to get some take-out.

This is it for me, this is like the final straw, I just snap, go

'Sammy, you said we'd only be here five minutes. It's been three hours.'

But he's all

'Babes, why you stressing, we just chillin'
gives me that smile.

So I says it, and I didn't want to, not in front of everyone but I'm done –

'We's supposed to be saving, Sammy, int we? That's what you told us. How we gonna move to London with you spending all the money on donner, chips and naan.'

He laugh at me then.

Loudly.

They all do.

I don't like it, the laughing, it make me feel weird. I can feel my face going red –

so I looks at him straight-faced.

'Sammy, you know I ain't joking.'

And he looks at me, sharp, his eyes at my eyes and goes 'Yeah. I know.

That's why it's funny.'

A sudden shudder comes over her whole body. She puts her head in her hands as if she is having a head rush.

The sound of birds and a heart beating, from the beginning, plays momentarily. She shakes her head, trying to delete the image and the sound. It builds to a crescendo, then stops abruptly. She gets her breath back, looks at us, a bit embarrassed.

It just the pills, the ones that Sammy give me so that I can sleep. They're strong. Make me feel crazy.

The sound of a car driving past once more, again she looks to the window, red and blue lights wash over her. She walks over and closes the curtains.

Morning coming.

She gets out her phone, holds it in her hand. She thinks a moment, wondering whether to dial the number.

I just wanna try him one more time.

She waits.

I can try him again, can't I? It ain't no big thing to try him again.

She waits.

There was no one there when I woke up.

I called him.

I wasn't sure if I shoulda, but then… three in the morning.

I left the house. I walked for ages.
The thing about town at that time is it's empty. I mean totally.
You reckon they'd be people wouldn't you? Odd ones, like
people who been pissed-up, drinking, or those mad old men that
always take their dogs out for walks when they can't sleep, or
workers on the night shifts, or postmen or police, even police,
you reckon you see police, or at least the odd car but it ain't.
It's dead.

Don't even see no cats.

I thought I was lost at one point, lost in my own home town,
how mad's that?

I only had my heels and they rub up my feet something proper.

She shows us the cuts on her feet.

It hurt. I think of my mum then. It's weird, cus for the first time
I don't think of Sammy, I just think how bad I miss her, I think
about Kevin – how he always tell me I can speak to her, and
how I always tell him that's bullshit cus you can't say nothing
to someone who ain't even there can you?

But sometimes,
when it's night, I hear him talking to her, I can hear what he's
saying, how he always tells her he's sorry. And that he's trying,
but it's hard, it's so hard.

I feel bad then, I think how much I wish I could go back, turn
myself backward, if I could just have one moment, one, just one
hour
to sit with her again, and she stroke my head and her hands
being so soft and warm and crinkly like paper

and her smell
like open windows after rain,
And biscuits,
And leaves.

Pause.

It start to rain.

Heavy, how it do in summer.

Look at my feet and see blood running red and filling up my shoe and the gaps between my toes.

Water's dripping from my eyebrows, touch my face and my hands come away black from where the mascara ran.

Feel cold then. And I think of Charlie. I imagine her all wrapped up in her bed asleep. I think about what she'll say when she wake up, I think about who gonna get her dressed and make her breakfast?

I don't know why but I worry what if I never see her again. And the thought of it make all my bones go to mush.

I sit down on the pavement. Look at the skin on my arms, and on my legs and it gone all chicken with the cold.

Swear, if I ain't had Sammy's jumper I think my nipples woulda fallen off. It can happen, I ain't lying.

I know it cus Carla told us.

She smells the jumper.

I smell Sammy's jumper and it smell like him.

Kinda sweet, but also musty, like
rooms with no windows.
It strong.

She smells it again.

Make me feel a bit sick, so I have to wait till I get my breath back again.

She smells it again.

Think it his.

Pause.

Think it smell like him.

It was just on the floor when I woke up, and it was the first thing I seen. Must be his, I mean –

Beat.

Who else's it gonna be?

She laughs, a moment of half-realisation spreads over her, as does the feeling of nausea. She runs quickly over to the bin, and begins to hurl. She throws up, once. When she is finished she slowly places the bin back down. She puts her hand inside her mouth and pulls out a single feather. She looks at it in her hand, then looks at us. Serious.

Can I tell you somethin'? You have to promise not to tell no one.

On Friday, just gone
when we left that party, after I seen the girl, with the scratches on her face…

We come back here, Sammy say he have to check something. I sit in the car on my own, and I don't know why I do –

But I do.

I look in his wallet, at his licence, and it say on it… it don't say Sammy, it say… It say Sammy's not his name. It say he don't live near Asda, it say he don't even live in Sinfin.

I feel sick, I think it just must be cus I smoke so much, cus it ain't even like it a big deal is it? I mean, what does it even matter?

Sammy come back and he see me with his wallet.

He don't say nothin' he just takes it off me, puts it in his pocket.

We drive in silence all the way home.

When we get to my house, I say 'Sammy, I don't wanna go home, I wanna stay here, I wanna stay with you.'

He don't say nothin'.

So I say to him again,
'When can we go to London?'

And he look at me 'You wanna go to London?'

'Yeah.'

'Really, you really wanna go?'

'Yeah, Sammy, of course I do, you know I do.'

And then his eyes go dark, and he say 'Well you best keep your nasty beak out my biznis.'

She shudders.

My head hurts. I always get headaches when I been crying. It's Kevin's fault cus of earlier, and you can tell him that if you see him, tell him Leah got a bolt through her head cus you made her cry so bad.

She rubs her head.

I shouldn't say shit like that.

I wonder what he's doing? Probably out looking for me, probably gone and called the police.

I wonder where Charlie is. Who's lookin' after her.

She really looks at us a moment, really studies us.

Sometimes… no.

She turns away, composes herself, looks back to us and speaks in one quick breath.

Sometimes when I look at her, I see all the things she is and all the things she's gonna be, and all the things I want for her and all the things I'm scared of and all the ways I love her so much that I think could just die for her right now and I wouldn't even care and I wouldn't even think nothing, and I think how did someone so little like her, and so full of just
goodness
come out from someone so broken, and the thought of it
the thought of it
the thought of it
makes me
just

Ache with, all these feelings for her. This…

Pause. Then quieter.

I remember when we went to Skeggy. Went to the caravan, and she woke up, cus Mum had gone out. Gone with no shoes on, and Kevin had gone looking for her, and she'd had this dream…

And she'd woken me up, come got in my bed. And she asked me why Mum was always going off, and I give her a cuddle, and told her what Auntie Maureen told me, 'bout the wounds that people have inside their heads.

And we went out, we went looking and when we couldn't find her we sat in the sand, and we looked out and all the sea being so black, and so big 'big enough to swallow a person' I thought and we didn't say nothing, but we knew. Charlie was only four, but we knew, we knew. We knew.

Pause. She scratches her head. Looks at the window.

I need to sleep.

She shakes her head.

When Sammy get here, and we go in the car, I'm gonna sleep all the way to London.

A pause, the idea of leaving Charlie is suddenly very painful. She shifts guiltily, can't look at us.

Beat.

She shakes her head and pulls herself back together. She turns to the window, and runs her hands over her head and stretches her body out. It is lighter, still and her body casts the shadow of a huge bird behind her. She touches her hair, her face, looks at her hands.

Man, I need to hurry up. Sammy be here soon.

She runs over to her bag once more.

This time she pulls out a pair of underwear covered in blood. She pauses with them in her hand. She stands quickly and moves over to the kitchen area – she shoves the underwear in the microwave, and slams the door. She finds her make-up bag and opens it. She takes out a mirror and looks at herself. She is slightly shocked by her appearance but she doesn't dwell. Tries to laugh it off.

You never tell me I look this bad.

She sort of laughs, sort of doesn't. She takes out a wipe and begins to clean her face, slowly and methodically.

You know, I been thinking. Today is the longest day ever for me. To me, today is a thousand years.

I been thinking how different today coulda been.

If I'd just gone to school, gone sat in class, all day, in the heat and windows all closed, in geography, and...

If I hadn't gone met Carla, hadn't told her 'bout Sammy, what we's gonna do tonight –

and.

If she hadn't said that stuff. The bad stuff, just
them

lies.

She throws down the face wipe. As she talks, she takes out some foundation and begins to apply it roughly. As she continues she applies lipstick, blusher, etc.

All that
shit
'bout him and his mates and

If I hadn't got upset. Gone home.

And –

if Kevin hadn't been in. Hadn't seen me. Hadn't shouted, said he was calling school, and all this shit 'bout being so worried, and how he don't know what to do with me, and what would Mum say and how he can't deal with me, he can't deal with me no more, he just can't deal with me, he can't deal with me, he can't deal, he can't –

If I hadn't left. Packed my bag. Put on my dress. Gone to see Sammy. At his house, his actual house where he live,
in Cavendish.

Music, gentle. LEAH *moves around the room, she picks up a bowl of water, and pours it over her head, as if washing herself.*

She looks at us, dripping with water. The sound of birds' wings, very very low.

I stand there, all the rain pouring down my face and in my hair.

I can see him through the window, there's some woman, and he's talking to her, look like he's shouting and she push him, she push him hard, away from her, and he grab her, he take her face, he try and hold her, but then she –

Come to the door, open it.

She run outside, and I hear him shouting so loudly inside the house, I hear him but I don't know what he's saying and I

See her.

The woman. She got big eyes, and her face is so full of sadness.

And I think – it his sister.

Must be his sister.

And there's this lump, in my throat and it's getting bigger, I think it's his –
Sister.

Must be, sister.

Must be his…

The birds' wings get very slightly louder.

And she's walking on the street now, and Sammy's come out after her, he's still shouting, but she's walking like she's in a trance and her face is so full of sorrow, that just for one moment I want to touch her, I want to just… put my hands on her and tell her it's okay, it's okay –

And that's when I see him. The boy. He's run out after her, on the pavement and the cars are coming so fast and he's running, and I think of Charlie, he's only little, I think of her, and he's run into the road, and the cars are coming so quick, and I'm running after him, and the cars are swerving, and he's still running, and the cars are skidding now, they're skidding, and I got my hand on his shoulder and I think of Mum.

I think of Mum.

And just then he shouts out –

Beat. The wings stop. LEAH *pauses painfully at the memory of what was said.*

They all stop.

This boy he turn
right round in the road and he look at me, really see me, like I see him and his eyes they're bright, green just like Sammy's.

I feel my skin go chicken, I wish I wan't wearing what I'm wearing and I know Sammy's eyes like stone on me too and I look up, I look up, I look up to see him and he's staring and the look, on his face and in that stare…

She looks at us. Lights dim slightly. Images of the city at night are projected on the walls around the flat as LEAH *talks – buildings, car parks, roads, houses, parks…*

I walk away fast.

I don't know where I'm going, I'm just walking and the noise of my heart in my chest and in my head is just…

I feel like I walk for hours 'fore Sammy find me.

He pull up and open the side door, but he don't say nothing. I get in.

We drive for what seem like for ever. Through all the city, buildings, shops, parks and…

We're back there. The house. Brown wallpaper. Spiral carpets.

We go in and all the men sitting round, like last time.
one
two
three
four
five.

Feel them look at me and my stomach turn.

We go upstairs.

Music begins to get louder.

It's dark. Musty. A room with no windows.

There's a mattress on the floor and a blanket laid on top.

He tell me to sit and I can feel the fabric through my dress, scratch up my skin and make me itch all over.

I look at Sammy
'When can we go London?'

'Soon. Soon.'

He gives me a pill –

'to help you sleep'

He take my cheek, strokes it gentle
with his
fist.

Tell me to take off my clothes, and I get beneath the blanket.

Music loud, dark, low and thumping, beneath it, wings and a heartbeat. LEAH looks at us in the half-light, she wipes her hand across her mouth, smearing her lipstick across her face. She drags her fingers, like claws down both cheeks.

The music gets deeper. Strobe lighting illuminates her, and the scratches down her cheeks glow UV. The underwear in the microwave also glows UV.

LEAH slowly takes off her jumper to reveal large bruises on her upper arms and thighs, and around her face and neck, they also glow in the lighting. Her body has become a crime scene.

She pulls her jumper high over her head, it is silhouetted against the wall behind her in the shape of a huge dark bird. She tosses it onto the floor –

The sound of flapping and squawking returns but this time louder. Underneath the sheets, huge birds begin to pull and struggle as if they have been trapped.

LEAH looks right at us in the half-light.

And when I sleep, I dream of birds, flying, struggling, chasing
round the room
I dream of Charlie, when she got born. How small she was, how
I held her
I dream of dancing on the benches and the world spinning
round me
I dream of Carla and her eyes like stone
I dream of laughing, filling up my ears and my head
I dream of the girl, and the marks like claws down her cheeks
I dream of the old man and his hand on my leg
I dream of the city at night, dead as a ghost
I dream of Mum, and how I miss her
I dream of Sammy, his hands on my body and my face
I dream of
His hands on my body and my
I dream
His hands on my body, my face, my
I dream of
Hands on my
Hands
I dream
Hands on
I dream hands on

me.

The music reaches a deafening crescendo. Lights snap up.
LEAH *looks up, she sees a bird in the sky.*

*The room has now become a wide expansive beach, the sea and
the horizon are projected on the walls around the flat, and
across* LEAH's *face. Huge wind turbines can be seen whirling
in the distance. Waves crashing, birdsong.*

I am eight.

And it's May time, I come home from school crying, cus some
boy called Ricky called me fat.

And you scoop me up, and say, I shouldn't listen to him, cus he
probably jealous, cus he knows I'm too clever. I don't say
nothin', and I know that you know how I feel, cus your face

look just like mine, and you say 'Tomorrow, let's go away, the two of us.'

'Just for a day', you say, 'just for one day, let's do it', you say, 'let's get the train, we can make us sandwiches' and I tell you 'we can't Mum, cus I have to go to school', and you say yes we can Leah, I'll call them up and tell them,
'you gotta live while you're alive, haven't you?'

And so we go, we get the train, all along the coast, and the sun streaming in through the windows,
and then we're sat there on the beach, with all the wind blowing.

You dig your fingers in the sand, and let the grains fall through them.

And you tell me you got something to tell me, and it's big news, cus now that Kevin moved in, everything's gonna be different. You ask me if I like him, and I tell you 'he's alright'

And you smile and say, that I'm gonna have a sister, and she gonna be called Charlotte, but I can call her Charlie, if I want to for short.

You stroke my hair, and your hand is warm, and soft and crinkly like damp paper

I put my head on your belly, close my eyes and imagine a heart beating.

And then you say you know that things been bad, for a while now, and that you're sorry, but you got a feeling, and it's a good one, like a little light inside you,
you say it feel like hope, you don't know why, but it just do. It just do.

And I smell you. Your smell like biscuits and leaves and fresh air after rain.

And we sit there, and the sun pouring down on us, and the waves crashing.

We sit there.

We sit there.

Beat.

And then we go home.

The projection of the beach suddenly cuts out.

LEAH *looks to the door.*

Beat.

Blackout.

End.

GYPSY GIRL

Gypsy Girl was first performed by Laura Lomas at Soho Theatre, London, on 5 October 2009 as part of Paines Plough's LATER programme.

I met Hayley in the summer. I always thought she was older than me but she wasn't. She just looked it.

You'd see her down Sev's by the benches, and she'd have a fag in one hand and a tin in the other. She had this look about her, like you would not fucking mess with her and if you did. She'd smack you, or get her sister to smack you. An' her sister was older.

With massive tits.

I never knew why she spoke to me. I was short and awkward with shit clothes.

I think she liked that.

An' I thought she was amazing.

We was always out down Sev's.

They had these swings and this shitty old roundabout that didn't even work, but we'd sit there, and smoke. And wait till the light was turning. And it was then you had this feeling, like, you didn't know why you was there and this sickness like, you should probably just get yourself home now. But you always waited. It was like a test. Even when it was cold and bitter or pissin' it down. We'd just sit there, on these swings. And pretend like we was alright with the world.

Hayley talked all the time.

She spurted the most incredible amount of nonsensical shit that you'd ever heard. It was amazing.

You never believed what she said. That's because it was usually a lie – but you listened anyway.

You'd shut your eyes and hold your breath for the things she told you.

She was that sort of girl.

She lived on the Caxton estate with her mum and her two sisters. They kept horses. It was weird cus their house was full of all sorts of shit. Nothing matched and everything stank. I hated going round.
I felt embarrassed.
Hayley's dad had died when she was younger and her mum was always talking about him. Stepping into the house you felt like they'd never really got over the shock of it, it was like a bomb had gone off and they'd just lived there, for years in the sort of chaos and debris of the aftermath.

They spent the money from the will on a little plot of land out near Finden. They had two horses. We used to go down on our bikes. We'd go over Sinfin bridge – and out past the canal and all of a sudden you'd be on dirt tracks and the landscape would just change, everything seemed to get massive and the colours of things would just smack against each other like they'd gotten brighter, more brilliant.

And we'd climb inside that field. There was a caravan that used to belong to her dad, it was falling into pieces, all twisted, cracked glass and broken plastic, but Hayley loved it. And it's true, there was something peaceful about the place. You could hear the water streaming in the river half a mile off.

You could watch Hayley there, and something different in her. Something quieter. She didn't talk that much, she'd just stand stroking the animal or sit for a bit and draw with sticks in the dirt. I always thought she belonged there, you know how people do. I was never so sure about myself but Hayley. She belonged there. She looked like a gypsy in the amber light. She was always so still with them horses.

Outside that field she was like a rocket fizzing up. All red fire and spilling over. Sometimes when she spoke she'd get so angry that she'd just be spitting the words out.
All this strangled life inside her.

It scared me.

She used to smack things. Broke her hand once for smacking it
so hard against this wall.
All cus some lad had called her fat.

And after she sobbed these big silent tears. Her whole body
heaving, like she'd forgotten how to breathe and was just
aching for air,
or a touch.

Something.

I don't know what.

It was a Sunday when we met them.

We'd been in the park as usual and Hayley was motormouth-
telling me how she'd met some footballer from Queens Park
Rangers and how he'd asked for her number and kept calling
her and everything.

All of this lies but I was sat there listening and thinking how
wide and white her eyes were when she talked. Dragging my
heels in the dirt and looking at the sky. And next thing I'm
looking up and there's these two lads stood high above us, and
grinning. And all...

'What's your names then?'

Hayley's silent. Not motormouth no more. She's still and
smiling going

'Hayley. Why? What's yours?'

'Mark', he goes. 'And your friend?'

'Lucy.'

And the other one, Ian. He smiles at me. And it's this smile that
makes me feel like I've swallowed my own stomach, cus I
know where this is going. And I know I'm going with it.

We get in the car. This souped-up Ford Fiesta bastard. All tinted windows and lowered suspension.

Hayley's in the front with hers. He puts on some music and we roll out, across Sinfin bridge, over the canal and onto the dirt track, where the light shifts and the colours smack against each other.

But then we start doing sixty. And the car isn't rolling now. It's bouncing, thundering through the dirt tracks and I can feel my blood going, it's racing through my body like a current. Like I'm made of wires, all taut and static. And Ian passes me a spliff and grins a gold-toothed grin. And it's now that I feel it. I look out the window and the colours are all wrong. Not smacked against each other now. They're rolled up and bound together and bleeding into one.

Hayley's laughing and squealing in the front, hers is looking at her and grinning and putting his foot down when she laughs. Ian is drinking from a can and passing it me, rocking back and forth. He smiles, puts his hand on my leg.

'What you so scared of, eh?'

I smile too, an awkward backward smile that doesn't even belong to my face. I drink the cider, try to backtrack.

Then we stop. Turn off the stereo.

Get out the car.

And everything is dusky, amber. Shadows.

The horses are silhouetted against the caravan. Ian climbs over the gate and offers me a hand.

I look back and I can see Hayley with Mark, and he's got her pressed against the car, and her body's all arched and twisted out of shape. He's pushing into her like she's made of nothing, clay. And she's laughing, but I swear she don't like it cus she's pushing back against him and her foot is tapping in the sand.

Ian's got my hand and he's pulling me harder toward him.

'Wait a minute.'

But he's got me by the wrist.

'Leave 'em to it.'

Mark's got his hands on Hayley's face now, and he's pushing her forehead into the tinted glass. I can see her shoulders heaving as he pulls away, and keeps his hand there on her forehead for a moment

then runs his other one down her throat.

She smiles, a half-smile, that's set all wrong on her face.

He says something, and leads her off toward the caravan.

'You alright Hayley?'

'Just fuckin leave 'em, will ya.'

She's got her head down as he walks up the steps.

'Hayley! Hayley!'

Ian squeezes my wrist, fingerprint bruises on my arm. I turn and pull and I'm free and I'm running. My legs like motors, I can hear the water, it's filling up my ears and my head. And Hayley is stood on the steps, and the sun's stretching out across her face.

She looks at me.

'Just leave it, Lucy.'

She walks inside the caravan. Mark closes the door behind them.

I can see her face, full of shadows. She looks filthy in the half-darkness. Like a gypsy, in the dirt.

'Hayley?'

But she's already inside.

He tightens his hand round her hair, loosens the buckle on his belt and pulls her face backward.

Through the cracked glass and split plastic, I can see her. She's got her eyes raised up to him. He's standing high above her. And her knees are dropping to the floor.

And I'm stood in this field and I feel like I'm just pouring. I'm flooded with something – I don't even know what.

And I'm shutting my eyes and holding my breath.

Thinking 'Breathe, Hayley. Just remember. Remember to breathe.'

WHERE I'M FROM

Where I'm From was first performed by Laura Lomas at Nottingham Playhouse, on 22 July 2010, as part of Paines Plough's 'Come To Where I'm From' season.

So I'm stood in this car park and he's not even turned up yet. The first proper thing I ask of him in two years and he can't even sort himself out to arrive on time.

Told him on the phone, when I spoke to him two weeks ago. Said 'Be here for ten will ya Jamie?'

And he's all 'Yeah. Yeah. Course I will.'

And I'm telling him 'It's important. Not to be late.'

'What do you take me for Kel?'

And I'm feeling guilty for doubting him. So I leave it. Put the phone down. Start counting down the days.

I didn't sleep at all last night. Not one bit. Just lay there looking at the plaster peeling off the ceiling.

Thinking of her.

'S like swallowing a knot.

I've been through it in my head. Everything. Told Jamie to bring us some clothes. Something smart. Simple. Cus you can't can you? Turn up looking like shit when it's been…

And and

You've got to look proper. And I will. I am.

It's twenty to eleven now, and everyone who's been has gone. Fucking November and I'm stood in the car park, in nothing but my T-shirt and joggers.

She's looking at me. The guard. She has been for ten minutes.

'You alright Kelly?'

'Yeah. I'm fine, thanks.'

'Got someone coming for you?'

'Yeah.'

'Late are they?'

I don't answer.

'Do you want to come inside?'

She thinks he's not coming.

I shake my head.

'You sure Kelly?'

'I'm alright,' I tell her. 'My brother's on his way. He won't be long.'

She stalks back inside. And shuts the door behind her.

He'll be here soon. He's probably just got lost. Took a wrong turn or something.

I wait a bit longer. Shut my eyes and think of Emily.

I never knew I was pregnant. I never even thought it. And the stillness when I found out. And I remember cus I'd just got the flat, and thinking it was the first place that had felt like a home.

And then

Me alone in this doctor's surgery. Buttoning up my jeans after the nurse has gone, and he comes back in. He's embarrassed cus I'm not quite finished, and he's awkward and sorry but he's got the results of my test, and did I know I was? And do I need advice?

I remember walking round all afternoon. It was summer. And feeling more alive than I had done in years. And after everything, all that time in Rose Hill Street, digging my claws into the walls.

It was like being made new. Like being washed or. Something. I don't know…

And that she was healthy was…

I remember her tiny fingers, wrapped around my thumb. And this feeling spreading over me. An aching. Like a bruise.

Two hours later we're on the motorway. Jamie's car's still in the garage, which is why he's late he says. Had to ring up Steve and ask to borrow his. Steve has a red Ford Fiesta, that smells of fags and dogs. There's empty beer cans and sweet packets on the floor. The heating broke last summer so it's colder in than out.

It's a miracle it moves at all, but it does and we're doing seventy down the M1. Jamie passes me a blanket. It's covered in dog hairs and smells like old sweat, but it's better than nothing. I tell myself.

I can tell he wants to say something but he doesn't know what.

He puts the radio on, and we both sit there listening for a while. Some bullshit song by Cheryl Cole. I turn it off, and then there's the silence.

My skin prickles.

He asks me 'how I'm feeling?'

'I'm fine.' I tell him.

Says he saw Sophie down the pub and she was asking after me.

'That's nice.' I say.

'She says you can stay with her. For a few weeks. If you need?'

'No thanks. Gonna get me own place. Gonna need it soon. I've got a number to ring first thing in the morning. It's family housing.'

'Right' he nods. 'That's good.'

Then. 'Kelly…'

But he doesn't finish.

I look in the back.

'Did you bring my clothes Jamie?'

'Forgot them.'

He stares straight ahead.

'I asked you to bring them, Jamie. What the fuck?'

'You don't have to swear.'

'It was the only thing I asked of you.'

'Alright Kelly. I forgot.'

'We need to stop and get something. I can't go like this.'

'Where?'

'Go to a Tescos, anywhere. Doesn't matter does it.'

'I've got no money.'

'So?'

'Are you serious?'

I don't answer.

'It'll be okay. You look fine Kel. She won't even notice.'

I look out the car window. Press my face to the glass.

Ninety miles to go. I drift off into sleep.

You're four years old, and you've got your arm wrapped tight round my leg. We've walked from the flat to Markeaton. We brought a loaf on the way. Twenty pee from Co-op.

We're stood at the edge of the pond and lobbing crusts at these ducks. They're squawking and you're laughing. And we finish off the loaf and walk over toward the mini-golf. You want to play but I can't afford it so I tell you we can do it next time. And you're happy, you seem alright with this. And I brush through your hair with my fingers and tie it up out your face. You want a French plait but I don't know how to do them so you settle for a bun. And I buy you an ice cream, and we share it. And we have a ninety-niner with a flake and chocolate sauce and we melt Skittles on the top. And you get it all down your chin, and on your new dress. But I'm not angry, and you knew I wouldn't be. And I lick my thumb to wipe your chin clean. And you go on the spider frame, and you race to the top, and I worry you'll break your arm, or your leg. But you're fine. And you're waving. You're waving. And I'm smiling, and I'm waving back

And we're normal. The two of us. For a day, we're just like that. Just like normal.

When I wake we're twenty miles out of town.

Jamie's in a service station, I can see him through the window, he's buying crisps and a can of Coke. He's left the car running, and the whole thing is rattling.

He climbs back inside, throws a packet of ready salted on my lap.

'Eat these.'

'I'm okay.'

'Eat 'em.'

'I'm not hungry.'

'You need to eat Kel.'

I say nothing.

Beat.

'Fine.'

He takes them back, and he's shoving a handful of Quavers in his mouth as we reverse around the corner.

M roads have changed to A roads. And I recognise the turnings. We've gone past Donnington, and the Francis Burdett. I remember it being run by gypsies. They had a massive dog that was always sleeping.

And sitting there with our dad. Him smoking packs of twenty, and giving us money for the two-pence machines. He'd burn her name into the plastic cellophane of his fag packet. And me and Jamie would pretend we hadn't noticed that his eyes were red.

I'm looking at Jamie and his eyes are on the road.

'Did you give her my letters?'

'What?' he goes. Mouth full of Quavers.

'That I sent for her. Did she get them?'

'Course.' He spits it. 'Told you that already.'

And his gaze is fixed forward as we turn onto the ring road.

Last time I saw her she was six years old. Linda brought her in, which was good of her. Cus there was a time, when things were bad between us that I didn't think she would.

And after everything. And even then to bring her in. I felt... I was very grateful.

She dressed her in leggings and little red shoes, with this long yellow T-shirt that had this slashed off-the-shoulder neck. I didn't like it, it was too grown-up. She looked all wrong and out of sorts.

They don't let you touch them. That's the hardest thing. You're sat opposite this little thing, and she's halfway off her chair, she's pushing dirt around the floor with the tip of her toe. And you're talking to her. 'Emily, how you doing sweetheart? Emily.'

And she won't look at you.

And she's scared of you.

And you can't even reach out to touch her face.

That's the thing that kills you.

I told her not to bring her again. Couldn't put her through it.

Checking her shoes, and inside her mouth. Not right for a little girl.

Not for mine anyway.

I've still got all the letters. Kept them in a box under my bed. Few pictures, drawings that Linda sent me.

Didn't look at them, that much. Was enough for me. Just to know that they were there.

We're getting closer now, and I can feel this thumping in my chest. We drive past the old hospital and Sainsbury's where I worked for a while when I was still at school.

I pull down the mirror, and look at my face. My skin's a bit blotchy but it's not too bad. Put my hair up in a pony, and tie it with a bobble.

Not the best but it'll do. And Jamie's probably right – you won't even notice that much. Probably not at all.

And later I'll take you to the cinema. We can see whatever you want. And it won't matter what it is, but to sit in the dark and just be quiet with you for a while. Like before, in our flat. When you'd fall asleep in front of the telly. And that'll be enough. For me. That'll be it.

Jamie's missed the turning. It was half a mile down the road.

'Jamie, you've missed the turning.'

But he carries on.

'Jamie?'

His eyes are fixed straight ahead.

'What you doing Jamie. You're going the wrong way.'

And he says nothing, and keeps on driving. But I know then, and there's this sinking, like I think I always must've known.

When he stops the car, he doesn't speak for a long time.

We sit there, very still. He's got my letters in a bundle on his lap.

'I didn't know how to tell you'

he says.

'Just wanted to get you home first.'

'Is it Linda?'

I say.

'Reckons it's too soon or something, cus it's not. Can't be soon enough.'

'It's not Linda.' He says. 'It was Emily's decision.'

I stare at the crisp packets and empty beer cans on the floor. There's a Skittle in the corner. I try and lift it with my toe.

When I get sorted. We can start over again. And we can live in a nice house, with your own bedroom, and a garden. And I'll cook you proper meals, and drive my own car, and pick you up from school, and wear nice shoes.

And go on holidays.

And we'll be normal. Together. That'll be us.

Other Titles in this Series

A Nick Hern Book

Bird and other monologues for young women first published in Great Britain as a paperback original in 2014 by Nick Hern Books Limited, The Glasshouse, 49a Goldhawk Road, London W12 8QP

Bird and other monologues for young women copyright © 2014 Laura Lomas

Laura Lomas has asserted her right to be identified as the author of this work

Cover image: Mandy Horton

Designed and typeset by Nick Hern Books, London
Printed in the UK by Mimeo Ltd, Huntingdon, Cambridgeshire PE29 6XX

A CIP catalogue record for this book is available from the British Library

ISBN 978 1 84842 463 0